'BIGFOOT SMELT OF PEANUT BUTTER'

Mountain climber Giglio Llamo of Palermo thought he was doomed when he became dislodged from his precipice and plunged nearly one hundred feet downwards into the trees. But help came from an unlikely source . . . one that isn't even supposed to exist.

'I thought I had broken my ankle,' he told a local pirate TV station after the experience, 'and then I heard the sound of something crashing through the undergrowth. When I finally saw what it was, I got the shock of my life . . . Bigfoot!' Llamo, twenty-eight, claims the huge creature lifted him to safety at the edge of a motorway, where he flagged down a passing car. 'Bigfoot was about eight feet tall and smelt of peanut butter,' he went on, 'and he told me never to go out climbing on my own again, before he went back into the forest . . . I'll never forget him.'

About the Author

Steve Wright was born and raised in South London. His father runs a tailoring business and his mother works for the Government. Steve has the fifteenth biggest nose in the country and is partially deaf in his right ear. Apart from a record 7.2 million listeners who tune in every day to his show, Steve Wright in the Afternoon, it attracts a number of big stars – Mick Jagger, Stevie Wonder and Terry Wogan to name but a few. Steve has held down a variety of jobs – singing on television commercials and jingles, and working as a British Telecom engineer, which was a success until they asked him to climb up telegraph poles.

Steve's show has been part of the national psyche for the greatest part of the decade. His show is continually voted the No. 1 radio programme in Britain.

IT'S ANOTHER TRUE STORY

Steve Wright

with

Richard Easter

Illustrated by Colin Yeates
Headlines by Cynthia Robinson

NEW ENGLISH LIBRARY
Hodder and Stoughton

Copyright © 1989 by
Steve Wright
Illustrations Copyright ©
1989 by Colin Yeates

First published in Great Britain in
1989 by New English Library
paperbacks

An NEL paperback original

British Library C.I.P.

Wright, Steve
It's another true story.
I. Title
823'.914[F]

ISBN 0-450-49474-8

Printed and bound in Great Britain
for Hodder and Stoughton
paperbacks, a division of Hodder
and Stoughton Ltd., Mill Road,
Dunton Green, Sevenoaks, Kent
TN13 2YA (Editorial Office: 47
Bedford Square, London WC18
3DP) by Richard Clay Ltd, Bungay,
Suffolk. Photoset by Rowland
Phototypesetting Ltd.,
Bury St Edmunds, Suffolk.

To Cyndi and Tommy

Riddle me this:
Where is my cat? (Answer within.)

A CRYSTAL BALLS UP

We've all heard of Nostradamus, the prophet who predicted, amongst many other things, the second and first world wars with frightening accuracy.

But less well-known is the fourteenth-century French prophet, Henri of Lyons. Like Nostradamus, Henri foresaw events by gazing into a bowl of water. But unlike his counterpart, Henri was only really any good at predicting totally mundane, useless things.

One of his prophecies went thus: 'Only six hundred years hence, there shall become shoes that shall be worn without aid of twines and shall be used by the sea and in the sun' – Henri had predicted flip-flops.

Other totally useless prophecies collected in his book, *The Seeing*, include ringbinders, the wok, fast-food restaurants, bucket shops and phone locks.

Mark D. LeBay, who has investigated the prophet at length, says in his book: 'Henri really was quite useless. He always seemed to miss the point. I mean, he predicted TV dinners . . . but not the TV. What a prat.'

HAIR TODAY, HORMONES TOMORROW

Since The Beatles, there have been many cases where a fan stops simply liking a particular pop group and becomes obsessed with them.

One such fan is Jenny Cunningham of Minneapolis, USA. She became a Prince fan in 1984 and has spent, in her reckoning, over $30,000 on her idol, including buying a bike identical to the one used in the Purple Rain film, and a complete wardrobe of copies of his clothes. But now she wants to look even more like Prince than ever before. She is taking a course of hormone treatments in order to be able to grow a moustache like the pop star's.

Her mother, Pauline Cunningham, says: 'Oh these youngsters! When Jenny told me she wanted treatment to grow a moustache I just laughed, but gave her the money anyway. It's only a phase she's going through.'

Jenny is fifty-two years old.

DEAD MAN DEFIES DESCRIPTION

A car crash on the Chicago Interstate Freeway last year involved ten different vehicles, but mercifully only one fatality – the driver who had caused the accident by veering across the highway in the face of oncoming traffic.

But problems started when the police arrived on the scene. Firstly, the car's registration produced no reaction when fed into the police computer. Secondly, the dead man had no ID. And strangest of all, police pathologists who examined the body found that the victim had two glass eyes and wooden legs – but real feet.

ORAL SAX INJURES MUSICIAN

You may have heard of the Jay Hawkins Jazz Quartet from New Orleans, the home of jazz itself, but you may not know that Jay Hawkins himself was nearly killed in a bizarre accident in 1951, just two years after the band was formed.

While playing at one of the city's premier jazz clubs, the 'Ten to Eight', Hawkins, then only twenty-two, fell from the stage while playing a saxophone solo. He hit the ground face first and, in a million to one accident, swallowed his entire saxophone.

The hospital was unable to operate straight away, preferring to see if Hawkins brought the instrument up naturally, but after two days, the decision to go ahead was taken.

'Many musicians feel that their instrument is part of them,' Hawkins said in a recent interview. 'And in my case, for two days, it was!'

MEAT PIES – AND EYES!

When his business of supplying ham and turkey rolls to vending machines began to fall through, Charles Stevenson took up a different kind of job . . . murder.

Forty-eight-year-old Stevenson would cruise the streets in his van looking for suitable victims, and would kill them using a cut-throat razor. Then he and his wife, ex-champion roller skater Hattie Pollop, would dispose of the bodies by using them as fillings for their meat rolls.

Using this method, their business picked up for a while, as using corpses for meat cut their overheads, but one day a customer found a set of false teeth in his roll.

At their trial, the judge described Charles and Hattie as 'evil, scheming, murdering scum', but congratulated them on their innovative use of free enterprise.

MAN LOSES HEAD TWICE

While visiting the alligator zoo in California, jobless Pablo Verucchi got too close to one of the exhibits, and had his head bitten clean off.

The two pieces of twenty-seven-year-old Verucchi's body were rushed to a nearby hospital where, in a pioneering ten-hour operation, the two sections were painstakingly reconnected.

When the young man regained consciousness, however, bad news awaited him. 'We are a private clinic,' said the doctor who performed the operation, 'and Mr Verucchi simply didn't have enough money to pay the fees. Sadly, we've had to disconnect our work.'

Despite protests from local action groups, the clinic remained steadfast. As the doctor told papers, 'We're a business, not a bloody charity. You can't just swan in and expect your head to be sewn on for nothing.'

SOLO LAUNCH!

Tragedy hit Japanese heavy metal band 'YYYING' when they began their first song at a packed concert hall.

The singer of the band, Ling Po, takes up the story: 'Our drummer, Zob, had just launched into a solo when he just . . . well . . . exploded.'

According to the medical report on Zob's death, the unfortunate drummer had played the exact note of his stomach's resonant frequency when he began to beat the bass drum. Just like a high note shattering a glass, Zob's stomach simply exploded. The rest of the band are taking no chances from now on . . . they play all their concerts from inside a sound-proofed box some miles away from the actual stage. 'You can't be too careful,' Ling Po said. 'One second you can be singing, the next . . . pow! You've gone out with a bang.'

LIVING WITH SPAM, A HELLUVA FEAT

Complaining of pains in his left foot, pensioner Phillip Staines of Chicago visited his local GP.

After examining the foot, the doctor proclaimed that the pains were a result of Mr Staines' foot being made completely of spam.

'I couldn't believe it!' Mr Staines said. 'In all my seventy-five years, my foot has never given me any cause to complain, and as soon as it does I find it's made of household meat!'

Several pet food manufacturers have expressed an interest in using Mr Staines' foot in their advertising, but he has refused. 'My foot's still my foot, no matter what it's made of,' he says.

"ANY EXCUSE TO GO
FOR A DRINK WITH THE BOY'S!..

MILDEW MAKES A MEAL OF MARK

Keen home-owner Mark Nicholson of Green Bay, USA decided to rid his windowsills of the mildew that had begun to grow on them, so one Saturday afternoon he and his wife, Sheila, got to work. Sheila takes up the story in a local newspaper: 'Just as Mark started to swab at the mildew with a damp cloth, it began to move . . . in a few seconds it had slid up his arm. After about half a minute, it had covered his entire body.'

Despite his efforts to remove the horrible living slime, it stayed fast on him and, in despair, Mr Nicholson ran out of the house.

'I haven't seen him since,' Sheila said, 'but it frightens me to think that my husband has become a horrible slimy mildew creature, and is roaming the country as I speak. Who knows what he'll do.'

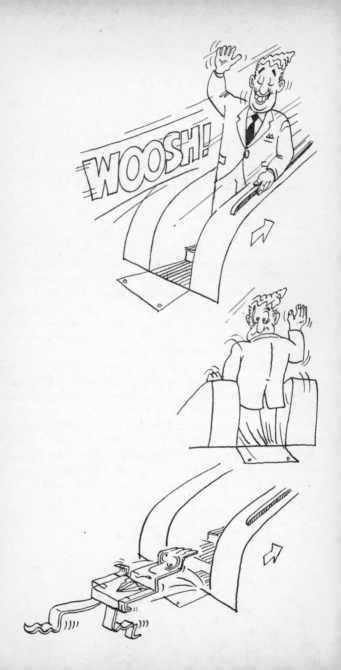

EVERY CLARKE HAS
A SILVER LINING

An escalator manufacturer lost a contract when one of their executives was accidentally minced while demonstrating the latest model, an American paper reported recently.

The escalator was designed to move at four times the normal speed of other types, and to show it off, forty-eight-year-old Robert Clarke insisted on being the first person to use it when it was installed in a large department store.

Mr Clarke stood on the bottom step, then gave the order for the machine to be switched on. Waving to the crowd, he sped upwards. Unfortunately, when Clarke – an ex-female mud wrestler – reached the top, his trousers got caught in the grille, and within seconds he had been sucked into the machinery and minced.

The company are said to be 'particularly upset' at Mr Clarke's death, but also 'very excited' at the prospect of re-marketing the escalator as a handy industrial tool for the meat industry.

PHEWEY – WHAT A SCORCHER

Lithuanian heavy metal band, 'Komisawa', started their tour with a bang – literally! For in a terrible mix-up, the band managed to wipe out both themselves and the hundred fans present at one of their gigs.

The band had been pretty unsuccessful in recent years, and decided to start one of their shows with an exciting series of explosions from phosphorous bombs, timed with music.

But at the explosives depot, one wrong signature on the receipt for the high-tech fireworks meant that instead of harmless sparklers, the band had atomic rocket boosters rigged up by mistake.

So when the first note of the concert was played, it triggered off a horrible nuclear explosion, destroying both the band, their fans and the hall they were playing in.

The band's record company decided not to release their projected single – a version of the Beach Boys' 'Wipeout' – because they considered it to be in 'bad taste'.

EAR'S A NEW FASHION

American schoolgirl, Penny Johnson, was furious with her parents for not allowing her to pierce her ears, so she defied them . . . in an ingenious way that has earned her over one million dollars so far.

The fifteen-year-old from Boulder, Colorado, used her skills as a sculptress to create perfect latex ears – with holes in the earlobes for studs, earrings and other fashion accessories.

'People can always tell when you're wearing false earrings,' she said, 'but my slip-on false ears fool everyone – and you can wear real earrings, too!' The false ears rapidly caught on with her schoolfriends. When her father – a dealer in rubberwear – saw them, he recognised their potential. Now the ears are available in different skin colours and Penny is embarking on a new venture . . . a false nose for people who want to wear nose studs.

YOU CANNOT BE SIRIUS!

The Yugoslavian town of Latvia had its very own super-hero . . . for two days. People in the town couldn't believe their eyes when self-styled superman, 'Captain Alarm', swept through the town dressed in a cape resembling curtain material and wearing a face mask that looked uncannily like a tassled lampshade.

'Captain Alarm' claimed to be from the planet Peeon in the Sirius System, and promised startled onlookers that he would rid the Earth of evil. However, when he offered to demonstrate his amazing powers by flying from the top of the hundred-and-fifty feet tall town hall, he plunged to the ground, killing himself instantly.

When the Burgomaster unmasked the Captain, his identity was revealed . . . Yut Fluge, an escaped inmate from the local mental asylum.

COWBOYS – 2
TOWNFOLK – 0

They say that crime doesn't pay. Well, for the Michaels gang of the old Wild West, it certainly did!

On June 8th, 1885, they robbed a national bank in Memphis, USA, and got away with nearly half a million dollars. To their amazement, when they ran out of the bank, they saw that the general store was being held up, too. Quickly ditching their haul in a safe place and ridding themselves of their disguises, they cornered the members of the other gang and handed them over to the police, thus claiming the $1,000 reward.

It was only afterwards that the real identity of the law abiders was discovered and a new reward offered for their capture!

LETHAL BACKHAND SHREDS UMPIRE

Do you take sport seriously? Surely not as much as Madeline De Passant of French Canada.

In a heated argument with the umpire during a tennis match at her local sports club, she struck the unfortunate man over the head with her racket.

By an incredible fluke, the wires of the racket went straight through the man's head, reducing it to slices like cheese through a grater.

De Passant, thirty-six, admits to manslaughter but denies intent to murder, adding: 'How could I plan to mince a man's head with my tennis racket? But it was a damn good shot, don't you think?'

SECRETS OF A
MIDNIGHT DRESSER

Here's a truly crazy true story!

Like millions of people, Tony Miretti of Toronto, Canada, goes to bed naked, but that's where the similarity stops . . . for he always wakes up clothed.

'It's strange but true,' the confused man told a New York paper. 'I don't sleepwalk, but every morning I wake up with four or sometimes five layers of clothing on!'

But the truly weird thing about the affair is that none of the clothes belong to Miretti himself. 'Where do they come from?' he wonders. 'Maybe somewhere else in the city people go to bed clothed and wake up naked!'

Police say they are 'baffled but amused'.

SPACE ALIENS DO IT AGAIN

It seemed that disaster was imminent when mountain racing driver Sean Croning of Elko County, Nevada, nearly plunged over the edge of a cliff while driving in the mountains.

Just as it looked as if the car would topple headfirst down the steep rock face, the back wheels caught on a sharp jutting boulder, which left the car hanging precariously.

'All it would have taken was a fairly strong gust of wind and I would have crashed over the side. I thought my luck had run out,' he said afterwards.

'But suddenly the sky was filled with a bright red light, and when I looked up, I couldn't believe my eyes. It sounds crazy, but there floating above me was a giant spaceship.' The thirty-two-year-old claims the alien craft sent out a 'force beam' which pulled the car back onto the road.

'I owe those space aliens my life, but as soon as I was safe, the giant spaceship simply flew away,' Croning says, adding, 'but now I live in fear that they may return.'

FAKE LEG KICKS UP OWNER

One night last year, Oliver Schneider woke up to find himself being attacked . . . by his own artificial leg.

At 3.00 a.m. on June 5th 1988, thirty-eight-year-old Schneider felt himself being kicked repeatedly in the head. He awoke to find the plastic leg hopping around in the dim light, taking pot shots at him.

'There was no way it could move on its own,' he said, 'but yet there it was hopping round my room, attacking me.'

Thus began six hours of terror for the man, who was chased around the house by the animated prosthesis before he managed to lock himself in the bathroom.

Doctors say the bruises all over his body could have been self-inflicted, but seemed to match the kind produced by kicks. As Schneider has no history of mental illness and has no reason to lie, it seems that it really is another True Story.

MANURE À LA CARTE

They say that gamblers will do anything for a bet, but no one in their right mind would want to take up the wager that nineteen-year-old Alex Rice did.

Rice says he usually gambles with cards, but if the stake is high enough, he'll try anything . . . and that's just what he did when his workmates bet him £500 to eat two tons of cow dung – fresh.

Incredibly, the teenager managed this incredible feat in just under three hours, washing the horrible meal down with plenty of beer and water. Now he has gained more than just the money. 'It sounds disgusting, I know,' he told a local paper, 'but I've acquired a taste for the stuff. Now I spend at least a couple of quid at the stables down the road on horse manure . . . that's usually the best quality stuff.'

Needless to say, Rice has lost his job, his girlfriend and most of his friends.

STONEHENGE BURGER AND CHIPS, PLEASE

A German archaeological team have claimed that Stonehenge was more than just a huge sun-worshipping temple.

The Alt-Neubauten team from Köln say they have discovered bone and wood remnants that hint that in the distant past the monument was a form of ancient fast-food restaurant.

Carvings found in ancient rock slabs indicate that, rather than Druid priests, the white-robed figures were in fact an early version of the burger bar assistant.

IT WAS THE USUAL FIRST DAY OF THE
HANG GLIDING SEASON...

MAN-EATING HADDOCK MAY STRIKE AGAIN

The pursuit of adventure is often dangerous, but not usually in the way that hang glider Robert King found. While enjoying a flight one June afternoon, watched by his wife and son, he came face to face with a bizarre experience.

His widow takes up the story in a local newspaper: 'Rob was flying beautifully and I went to pick up our son, Timmy, so he could get a better look,' she said tearfully. 'When I turned round, Rob was flying directly into the jaws of what appeared to be a giant flying haddock.'

The unfortunate thirty-six-year-old was totally eaten by the strange creature which, Mrs King claims, flew off in the direction of Wigan. Although radar bases deny they saw any such large creatures on their screens that afternoon, the distraught woman has no doubts. 'A haddock ate my husband . . . God knows what it might do next.'

CHEAP AIR TICKET TAKES MISER ALL THE WAY

Miserly people try to save money any way they can, but forty-eight-year-old Guy Mills of Ontario, Canada, went just too far.

When the businessman read in a local paper that one of his local airlines was offering cheaper flights for disadvantaged people, he wasted no time in taking up the offer with a sneaky plan.

Wearing dark glasses and covering his eyes, Mills pretended to be blind on the outward bound flight in order to save money while visiting his sister. The plan went perfectly and he saved fifty dollars, but problems started when the skinflint tried to return home. Firstly, because he couldn't see anything, he boarded the wrong flight and ended up en route to the Antarctic.

Secondly, while trying to find the toilets, the modern Scrooge blundered against a badly closed door which flew open, depositing him in the jetstream and into the engines, where he was totally vaporised.

A RAVE FROM THE GRAVE

If you think you have no friends, then don't fret . . . you could be Simon Pack from Michigan.

One rainy night last March, police pulled the twenty-five-year-old over for driving without lights, and apparently carrying too many people. But when he wound down his window, they realised that the young man was surrounded by corpses, all dressed up in party gear, complete with hats and streamers.

The investigation into this bizarre situation revealed that Pack, having no friends because of a terrible halitosis problem, had raided the local morgue to find company for his birthday party.

When police investigated the strange man's house, they found over twenty-five corpses, all in various stages of decomposition, propped up in different poses all around the house.

Pack, a friend to the dead, was committed to a home for the insane.

EYEBROWS REVEAL ALL ABOUT MEN

If girls want to find out a man's most intimate measurements, then all they have to do is to look at his eyebrows, claims therapist Hanna Weisskophh.

For, in a study of the very vital statistics of over five thousand men, she found that the width of the eyebrows relates directly to the size of the genitalia.

'Men with very thin eyebrows are usually not particularly well endowed, but thicker and bushier eyebrows indicate that down there, there is something to be reckoned with,' says the cheeky forty-five-year-old.

'And if a man is effeminate enough to pluck the eyebrow, then the organ actually shrinks in size,' she claims.

Her revelations have led to thousands of American males embellishing their eyebrows with makeup . . . but the truth lies elsewhere!

'BIGFOOT SMELT OF PEANUT BUTTER'

Mountain climber Giglio Llamo of Palermo thought he was doomed when he became dislodged from his precipice and plunged nearly one hundred feet downwards into the trees. But help came from an unlikely source . . . one that isn't even supposed to exist.

'I think I had broken my ankle,' he told a local pirate TV station after the experience, 'and then I heard the sound of something crashing through the undergrowth. When I finally saw what it was, I got the shock of my life . . . Bigfoot!'

Llamo, twenty-eight, claims the huge creature lifted him up and took him over ten miles across the countryside to safety at the edge of a motorway, where he flagged down a passing car. 'Bigfoot was about eight feet tall and smelt of peanut butter,' he went on, 'and he told me never to go out climbing on my own again, before he went back into the forest . . . I'll never forget him.'

TIMESLIP

Here's an incredible story from the United States about a timeslip.

New York businessman, Richard Lawrence, buys a copy of The New York Times *every day at exactly 8 a.m., the American magazine* Incredible Worlds *reported recently.*

But last February, his regular paper seller was not in his usual place at the edge of 42nd Street and Madison, so Lawrence walked another block down to the next vendor. As usual, he purchased The Times *and put it in his case. But when he came to read the paper in his office, he realised to his amazement that the copy was eighty years out of date . . . from the year 1918.*

Checking with The Times' *offices, Lawrence discovered that reprints of the paper had never been available via a street vendor and certainly not in the pristine condition in which he'd purchased it. When he went back to the vendor to attempt to unravel the mystery, he got another shock – the old man had disappeared and shopkeepers in the area claimed that the last time a street vendor had occupied that position had been eighty years before . . . in 1918.*

SHOCK TURNS MIDGET GREEN

Sticking his hands into the electrical generator proved to be more than an electrifying experience for circus midget and trapeze artist 'Flying' Shorty Parker of Boston.

His friends in the 'Circus Humungous' dared him to place his hands in the huge petrol-driven generator, but when he did so, he received a huge electric shock. After being revived, Parker said he felt fine and capable of performing that night.

But during the midget trapeze act, which has made the 'Circus Humungous' world famous, Shorty's hands began to glow bright green, shocking his partner in the act so much that he lost control and fell into the lion cage where, tragically, he was partially eaten and died from horrendous flesh wounds.

BEAUTY AND THE BIRO

Here's one of the strangest fan clubs you'll ever read about!

If you find disposable ink pens exciting, adventurous and addictive, then you could do worse than to join the Yugoslavian fan club, 'Friends of the Biro'. There are over twenty thousand members all around the world and every month they all receive a newsletter detailing the activities of the world's most famous ballpoint pen.

'People say we're mad,' club chairperson Lechs Snorschoum says, 'but they can't appreciate the magic and beauty of the Biro.'

BALDMEN SAY STINKY POOPE REALLY WORKS

Bald men in Japan have discovered a way of getting their locks back . . . but they have to look ridiculous for up to two years in order to do it.

Japanese sailors found that wearing the rare seaweed known as Latts Sunge Poope on their bald patches caused the hair to grow back. But there are drawbacks to this miracle cure: firstly, the length of time it takes for the seaweed to work; secondly, the fact that the plant smells of urine; and thirdly, it is bright purple. But this hasn't stopped over one thousand Japanese men from placing a fresh frond of the plant on their hairless heads each day. The fact that it causes hair to grow everywhere else as well hasn't put them off, either. 'So what if I have hairy lips?' one user said. 'At least I'm not bald.' Quite!

THE STRAIN OF CONSTIPATION

If you're ever constipated, then don't worry. You're still better off than Parisian Paul de Patis, who was killed by his inability to 'go'.

De Patis was constipated for an incredible eight years, despite a diet rich in roughage. Hope seemed to be in sight when the unfortunate twenty-nine-year-old was selected to be a guinea pig for a new anti-constipation drug, called Minotopix.

De Patis, however, disregarded the drug company's instructions and strained away so hard that he literally caused his head to implode.

The drug is not yet available.

GREEDY GREENFLY
GULPS GIRL

Mr and Mrs Paul Marton of Innsbruck, Austria, lost their
three-year-old daughter in a bizarre gardening accident.

When Francine Marton wanted to go out and sit in the
garden with some honey sandwiches, the couple could
see no problem, so they let the little girl have her way.
However, when they checked on her just over an hour
later, they found that the bubbly little girl's head had
been eaten away. Sticking out of the neck of her pretty
pink dress was a bare skull.

Police believe that Francine fell victim to a particularly
vicious kind of greenfly who, on detecting the honey
sandwiches, descended on the little girl and ate up her
lunch . . . with her head too.

TALKING TULIP RECITES POETRY

Swedish female mud wrestler, Lotte Svregan, couldn't believe her ears when her favourite tulip began to recite passages from Marcel Proust's A la Recherche du temps perdu, *a newspaper reported recently. The attractive yet large twenty-nine-stone woman claimed that while watering the plant, it began to speak perfect French and, what's more, the passages it was quoting were word perfect.*

'It sounds crazy and I know no one will believe me,' she said. 'After all, how could a tulip read a classic French novel when I don't even own a copy?'

THE AMAZING
SNAKE CHARMER

Tribesmen of the Matutu tribe of Africa claim their warriors are being killed by a talking snake, an African TV crew discovered.

The snake, called the Woolutu by the natives, is apparently able to mimic exactly the sound of a man crying for help, thus causing passers-by to venture into the bush in search of the person in need.

However, once in the dense jungle growth, the people become easy targets for the impressionist snake whose deadly poison can kill a man within seconds.

Tribesmen claim the snake is also able to shout such words and sentences as 'Over here!', 'Please, I'm injured!' and 'Goodness, you'll never believe this!' in order to trick victims into becoming its next meal.

VAMPYRE

Practical joker, Simon Davies of California, decided to turn up to a party in a coffin, dressed as Dracula. A friend from a local crematorium loaned the twenty-five-year-old salesman a genuine pine coffin and agreed to drive him to the party after work.

Davies disguised himself as the vampire and settled into the coffin in the back of the hearse . . . but he never got to the party.

The joke was on him, as he had got into the wrong coffin in the wrong hearse, it was discovered later, and had been totally incinerated in the crematorium's furnace.

His friend said afterwards, 'Simon would have laughed . . . What a mix up!'

SPACE ALIEN'S BUNGLE KIDNAP

One of the most intriguing recent discoveries was made off the coast of Japan: a huge metallic domed structure, believed to be a flying saucer, corroded by many hundreds of years underwater. Divers involved in oil exploration in early 1986 came across the strange object and photographed it, but attempts to raise the forty-metre-wide object have resulted in the badly rusted surface flaking away.

Markings on the outside of the structure, which look like writing, have yet to be deciphered and Yoki Mamasaka of the Tokyo Institute says in his new book that 'It seems to me the only proof positive we have of an alien vessel'.

Still more intriguing is that underneath the strange craft are the remains of a junk, dating back to China's Ming dynasty.

'We have yet to ascertain how a Chinese ship, dating back many hundreds of years, could be found off the Japanese coast. It may well be that the alien beings had attempted to kidnap it and its crew, but crashed before escaping the Earth's atmosphere,' Mamasaka says.

DJ IN A SPIN OVER RECORD

A man who never made it into the world's book of records is DJ Tony O'Neal, known over the airwaves in his home town of Jacksonville as 'Sharp Tony "O"'.

The soul music fan was attempting to make it into the record books by broadcasting non-stop for an entire month and a half, from his small studio in Park Street. His only contact with the outside world was his air hose as food and drink was supplied from a huge larder and freezer installed for the record attempt.

Delighted listeners in the small town were treated to twenty hours of commercial-free radio a day as the zany DJ told jokes, read short stories and, most importantly, played all the hits.

But after just three weeks, people began to notice that O'Neal's behaviour was becoming increasingly bizarre. He began to report, in whispers, that a giant talking armadillo had managed to get into his studio and watch him from the corner. Likewise, at other moments, he would, for no apparent reason, begin to quote Shakespeare, claiming that the aliens who had invaded the town were unable to listen to it without experiencing pain.

The thirty-two-year-old refused to stop broadcasting, even when a local doctor and the police pleaded with him to give up as it was affecting his mental capability.

When the law enforcement team finally managed to drag him, kicking and screaming, from the building, it became clear that the only place O'Neal's record attempt would get him into was the local lunatic asylum.

ANOTHER HEAD IMPLODES, TRAGICALLY

Ever dreamt of being a superhero? Well, sixteen-year-old Charlie Brown (that really is his name!) of California became one for just a day.

Bet by his friend to drink the horrible, grimy water from a sewage outflow, Brown readily agreed to the five-dollar wager.

But unknown to the two boys, the liquid that Charlie drank also had some pollutants mixed in from a top secret research establishment, one kilometre up the river.

Somehow the strange contents of the dirty water re-acted with the young boy's bodily processes, and he developed, incredibly, what comic book readers would call 'superpowers'.

For the next few hours, Brown was able to fly up to forty metres at a time, leap over tall trees and bend thick metal bars with his bare hands.

His friend, Steve Masterton, who had set the bet, told a local paper afterwards, 'I know it sounds incredible, but Charlie was just like superman. I was a bit scared, but I guess I couldn't believe it myself!'

But the young man's supposed superpowers were

never properly investigated, for in an unforeseen side-effect of the process, Charlie's head self-imploded.

Head of police, Malcolm Brown, said in his statement, 'Superpowers – bullshit. That Masterton kid is just a lying poisoner who's trying to escape the consequences of manslaughter.'

The trial continues.

ANGEL DOSHES UP TRAMPS

Is there an angel in New York? That's the question that the residents of that city found themselves asking last Christmas. Louis Green, one of the many thousands of homeless New Yorkers, was approached last December 24th by a tall man in a pure white suit, and given an envelope addressed to 'L. Green' in spidery handwriting. When the intrigued tramp investigated, he found to his amazement that the envelope contained a cheque for a cool ten thousand dollars made out to Louis Green. Since that time, the man in the white suit has been seen fifteen times, handing out huge sums of money to those in need. Some say he's a wealthy businessman, fed up with the trappings of money. But as one of the tramps of Brooklyn told a New York TV station: 'If he ain't an angel, he should be one.'

FRED AND BARNEY ARE REAL – IT'S OFFICIAL

By an incredible coincidence, it seems as if the characters and places that make up the hit cartoon, *The Flintstones*, actually existed!

Cave paintings found in South Africa, which are believed to be nearly a quarter of a million years old, depict figures that bear an uncanny resemblance to Barney and Betty Rubble, Wilma and Fred Flintstone, and even Pebbles and Bam-Bam.

Professor Johann Botha says of the discovery: 'The likenesses are quite striking. Although the town of Bedrock is not shown, I think we can assume that whoever painted these pictures must have actually lived around such a place and known such people, rather than just making them up.'

When Professor Botha was asked if it was possible that other characters such as Bugs Bunny actually existed once, he told the investigator: 'Don't be so impertinent, young man, or I'll tan your backside for you, see if I don't.'

HIDEOUS SMELL
KILLS HUNDREDS

You will have heard about the 'Black Death' or bubonic plague that ravaged Medieval Europe. Less well-known, however, was the plague called the 'Black Breath' that surfaced around the sixteenth century in Italy.

Scientists today believe that it was a particularly virulent kind of halitosis, brought about by microbiotic infection of the tonsils.

Like microbes in the atmosphere can cause milk, cheese and almost any type of food to become rancid, causing a foul smell, the 'Black Breath' microbes that attacked the tonsils literally caused them to 'go off'.

When this happened, the victim's breath became so foul-smelling and loaded with germs that one sniff of it could kill. Luckily, the disease was confined to the area of Italy known as Firenzuola and the death rate never rose beyond a few hundred.

Doctors believe that all that was needed to stop the 'Black Breath' was a decent breath freshener, such as those found in any modern-day chemist.

A TRULY SAD ENDING

Fate, or coincidence, play a large part in all of our lives, but sometimes, rather than being just a conversation piece, they can be deadly.

In November 1944 during the Second World War, Commander Steven Laurel was put in charge of the placing of landmines under a dirt track which Intelligence reported would be used by a tank patrol within a few hours. The Intelligence report was correct and, thanks to the accurate placing of the landmines, four out of five Panzer tanks were crippled.

In 1985, Laurel, then seventy-six years old, went back to Germany to see once again the sites of his wartime service, and to remember his comrades. One of the places he visited was the dirt track, now tarmacked over, but still in a quiet area of the country.

Laurel decided that his wife should take some pictures of him standing on the road. She had only taken a couple before he had to step to one side to allow a car to pass. As the car pulled alongside him, there was an explosion which caused it to be thrown onto Mr Laurel, who was crushed to death. By the time emergency services arrived, the driver of the vehicle was also dead. An investigation revealed that one of the landmines Laurel had planted forty-four years previously had remained undisturbed, cushioned by watery earth and clay, and the hot, dry summer had once again made the explosive dangerous.

But even more incredible was that the driver of the car, whose vibrations had set the mine off, was Herr Halkett Van der Lube – the driver of the one tank who had escaped destruction all those years ago.

A NOT SO ARMLESS EXORCISE

Exorcising the ghosts of lost souls is a well-known part of paranormal activity, and it is one of the few meetings with the supernatural that the Christian church openly documents.

But like all things, even exorcism, which is strange in itself, can become even stranger. In 1984, Louis Springfield of Nashville lost his left arm in a bizarre accident. Doctors were unable to reconnect the limb with microsurgery and as is usual in these cases, the limb was burned. But that wasn't the end of the story.

Springfield began to complain to his wife that he was seeing the ghostly shape of an arm out of the corner of his eye. Doctors put this down to post-trauma stress, but as the days went on, Springfield became increasingly agitated, often waking up screaming in the night that his amputated arm had been grabbing at him.

Springfield's behaviour became increasingly erratic, with his moods swinging between paranoia and outright terror.

The ghostly arm that had been haunting the unfortunate man disappeared after his wife suggested an exorcism, arguing that the limb couldn't accept that it had been removed.

In a half-hour ceremony, a priest ordered the arm to be gone from this earth and the effect on Springfield was immediate. He began to sleep again and became progressively happier.

That was until last year when he was found collapsed in his back garden. Despite protests from neighbours that they had seen no one else with him all afternoon, police still maintain that Springfield had been murdered . . . strangled to death.

"SO WHAT TEAMS DO YOU SUPPORT? ROMA?
OR JUVENTUS?"

BEACH BOY'S GREATEST HITS

Is time travel possible? Marcus Kasparian, a welder from the east of England, certainly thinks so. For the eighteen-year-old, when on holiday in Italy, claims to have found himself transported back 1500 years.

'I'd been dozing on the beach for a while and decided to get up for a drink, but when I opened my eyes I realised to my shock that the area had completely changed – all the holiday-makers had gone and, worse still, the resort itself had been replaced by ancient-looking buildings.' Kasparian claims that, as he watched, five Roman soldiers came over one of the dunes, spotted him and, before he could run, captured and bound him.

Kasparian says that before he could work out what was going on, he was back on the beach in 1987. 'I know a lot of people think I was dreaming the whole thing, but when I awoke back on the beach, my hands and feet were still bound.

'It makes me wonder how many people who disappear have gone back in time, like I did, but failed to get back to the future again.'

WIFE SWOTS BUG PLOT

Some people go to extraordinary lengths to check up on their partner's movements when they suspect them of being unfaithful.

But one of the craziest plans of all came from Martin Wilder of Connecticut. Thirty-six-year-old Wilder began to believe that his wife was entertaining another man while he was at work. Rather than confronting her with his suspicions, he worked out a cunning plan to catch her in the act, the Connecticut Post reported recently.

He began to mishear things his wife was saying and sometimes ignored her completely. Other times he wouldn't answer the phone, saying it was so faint it must be next door's.

After a month or so of this, he spent several thousand dollars on an audio surveillance unit which allowed him to 'bug' his entire house and hear anything that was said within it.

He continued to act as if he were hard of hearing and then produced the final part of his plot – a mock hearing aid which would receive transmissions from the 'bugs', allowing him to hear things as they happened.

His idea was that, while at work, he could monitor his house and catch his wife with her supposed lover.

But he never got to put the plan into action as his wife applied for a divorce just one week after the equipment came into the house – but not because she had a lover. Mrs Wilder found the strain of living with a deaf man just too much to take.

HOT MONEY COOLS CRIME

Here's a spectacular invention that will put big-money thieves out of business! It's a new type of safe that can be installed in banks or armoured trucks to prevent robbers getting at the money.

If anyone tries to open the safe without using the correct procedure, the unit converts itself into a gigantic incinerator with the temperature inside rapidly reaching 10,000 degrees centigrade, before cooling rapidly with the aid of refrigeration devices. So when the would-be robbers manage to open the door, all they find are heaps of charred paper!

The creator of the new security device, Paul Rheingould, says, 'It's the best deterrent to robbery I can think of. I mean, for example, imagine someone trying to make off with the "Mona Lisa" and getting away with nothing but burnt canvas. You end up with nothing and that's exactly why my safe is so effective.'

RUSSIAN ROULETTE CIGARETTES
AND DARTS

SMOKING DART SCORES EVERY TIME!

Of all habits, smoking must be one of the most difficult to give up. There seems to be no foolproof and easy way of quitting for good. But if an American company, HabitStop, have their way, their invention will make people give up cigarettes – forever.

For their new brand of cigars and cigarettes have an important addition that would put even the most dedicated of smokers off their 'fix'. It's not a foul taste, or an inflated price, but something that is literally fatal.

For if you light up one of the company's 'Stop-for-Good' cigarettes, the flame sets up a chain reaction that launches a concealed poison dart, which fires straight backwards into your throat, killing you within minutes. Smokers have branded the invention 'despicable' but the company are not put off. It's their aim to have their special, fatal cigarettes planted at random within well-known 'name' brands, so that as their managing director says, 'Smokers will have to ask themselves as they light up, "Will this be the last smoke I ever have?"'

COP COMES OUT OF THE CLOSET

A series of murders in the small American town of Brook left the local Police Chief there, Benedict McCleod, puzzled.

Whoever had killed six teenage girls always managed to avoid the law enforcement patrols with frightening ease, sometimes getting away just minutes before the first officer arrived on the scene.

The murders had begun on October 6th, 1970, and seemed to show no signs of stopping by Christmas of that year. McCleod found it particularly distressing to find that no fingerprints had been left and witnesses could not be found. The only clue was that all the girls had been seen with an older woman just shortly before their demise. She was described as tall, with brunette hair, and almost all who had seen her said she had been wearing a floral print dress.

McCleod resolved to interview every woman in the town of that description. But before he could, he discovered the killer far closer to home. One morning he felt a compulsion to search through his wife's cupboard and found in there a brunette wig and floral print dress matching the description exactly.

At that moment his wife entered the room . . . and the secret came out.

McCleod, a schizophrenic transvestite, had murdered the girls while in a state of trance and unwittingly had been investigating a crime of which he was perpetrator.

PING PONG EYE
BALLS

Tripping down the stairs seemed like the end of the world for Simon Ashley of Illinois, for the accident caused his glass eye to pop out and smash on the floor. And worse than that, he was on his way to an important business meeting.

'I couldn't turn up to a shareholders' meeting with only one eye,' the forty-five-year-old told a local paper, 'so I had to improvise.'

Half an hour later, he had transformed a ping pong ball into a new left eye. The colour didn't quite match and it was a little wonky, but it was better than nothing at all.

The plastic, disposable eye so impressed Ashley's friends at his local One Eyed Club that they all wanted one. Now he runs a company turning out plastic throwaway eyes in a variety of colours and styles.

FRENCH BREAD CAPER CRUMBLES

Crime certainly didn't pay for one bank robber in France last year. Dressed in plain clothes, he calmly waited in line until he reached the front of the queue and then handed a note over the counter, reading:

'I HAVE A GUN. DO NOT MOVE OR ACT STRANGELY. FILL A BAG WITH AS MUCH MONEY AS YOU CAN AND HAND IT OVER. BE QUICK.'

Unfortunately for the criminal he had made one mistake. The note was written on the back of an envelope . . . and on the front was his full address. Police arrested him within minutes.

SQWALK LIKE AN EGYPTIAN

The Egyptian government is furious at proposals from a leading hamburger company to turn one of their largest pyramids into a huge fast food and leisure complex. The 5,000-year-old structure would have its insides completely removed and replaced with saunas, swimming pools, hotel rooms, bars . . . and of course a huge burger takeaway.

The sphinx outside the pyramid would have its face sanded down in order to act as a screen for a projection of a huge sign saying, 'WELCOME'.

Conservationists are opposing the takeover, which will cost the company a cool $300,000,000, but a spokesman from the burger corporation said, 'It's time these Egyptians started getting a sense of perspective. The pyramid has been unused for so long that they'll never find another buyer. The nearest place tourists can get a decent burger is miles away, and that's not good enough.'

CONGRATULATIONS IT'S A
8lb CHICKEN!!!

MAN GIVES BIRTH TO LIVE CHICKEN

Texas businessman, Hugo B. Fassbinder, was bet $100 to eat fifteen raw chicken eggs in five minutes. Unbelievably, he won the bet, but just three days later he began to complain of stomach pains.

The pains came and went, sometimes being quite severe. After a month or so, he decided that a trip to the doctor was in order.

The medicine the doctor prescribed had no effect, but a subsequent X-ray revealed an extraordinary sight!

Incredibly, one of the eggs Fassbinder had eaten contained a chicken which had begun to grow in his stomach.

An operation, which the surgeon described as 'the first caesarian section I've ever performed on a man' removed the chicken. It was nearly full grown and now Fassbinder keeps it in a cage back on his ranch.

'The whole affair's certainly put me off omelettes,' he says.

SPACE ALIEN IN LOVE TRIANGLE

Here's one of the strangest reasons for divorce we've ever heard.

John Cohen of Jacksonville, Florida, suspected that his wife was seeing another man behind his back. She often went out early in the evening and returned late, her face flushed and usually her hair awry.

So one particular day last March he decided to follow her, to check if she really was visiting a friend down the road at Brunswick.

Driving a hired car so she would not recognise him, he followed her along busy main roads and deserted back streets until she finally turned off the highway and onto a dirt track.

Sure enough, his wife was meeting someone else – but that 'someone' was not of this earth.

As the shocked Cohen watched, his wife was swept into the four arms of a huge green creature and taken aboard its huge flying saucer.

Cohen is now trying to find a lawyer who will represent him in the divorce, but is not having much success: 'They'd help me if my wife was seeing another man, or even another woman, but they say space aliens just don't count. What should it matter what planet he comes from – he's got my wife!'

But Peggy Cohen remains unmoved. 'Voltan is a better lover than John ever was. We're going to be very happy together.'

The trial continues.

ET WRITES HOME

The huge lines carved into the desert in Nazca form intricate patterns which can only be seen from above. Scientists often wonder how the ancient civilisation that made them had the technology to do so.

But England has its own strange lines that can only be seen from above, scientists claim. It may be just an incredible coincidence, Paul Bunson of New York says, but certain hedgerows in Yorkshire, when viewed from above, spell out strange messages.

In his forthcoming book, 'Messages to Space', Bunson claims to have seen, using a helicopter to fly over the area, sentences like 'The red men lie here sometimes', 'Come soon blue planet' and 'Return soon'. Despite the apparent nonsense of these, Bunson claims they have been placed there by space aliens in order to let us know of their existence. But farmers from the area, such as Arthur Vazey, say, 'I put those hedges there myself and I certainly didn't have any help from little green men.'

Bunson claims to have had no history of mental imbalance.

"CURSES!... ONLY A MINUTE *LEFT*!
AND HE'S NEARLY DONE!!"

FRANK IS BACK IN TOWN

Last year in Bolivia, the town of Magdalena was rocked by a series of grisly robberies. Between February and June, sixteen corpses were stolen from the local mortuary. The police were concerned not only for the distress that this was causing the relatives of the deceased, but also that there was a possibility that the bodies were being used in strange black magic rituals. The truth turned out to be far worse.

On June 24th last year, the police stopped a car with a faulty brake light heading along South Street. There were two occupants: a man, Doctor Pedro Cortez, a well-respected member of the community, and the body of Martin Ignacio, a twenty-four-year-old who had died just days previously.

When interrogated back at the police station, the horrible truth came out. Cortez had become obsessed with the idea of becoming a modern-day Frankenstein. He had been using parts of the cadavers to create a new being. He wanted to re-animate it by using varying types of radiation instead of electricity, the method used to create Frankenstein's monster.

Doctor Cortez was formally charged with the offences, and locked up, awaiting psychiatric treatment. But there was a peculiar end to this case. In his statement, the mad doctor described the processes by which he had re-animated the dead. When police examined his laboratory they found all the equipment he had described, but no body. Just a broken lock on the door – from the inside.

OVERACTING ALIEN LOSES CONTROL, KILLS 12

Before HiFi stereo sound and 90mm screens, movie makers used all sorts of gimmicks to make their pictures come alive. But none were more bizarre than the film 'Death Teenagers from Space' made in 1955.

Whenever the film was shown, the entire cast would appear in real life, making it a cross between theatre and the movies. At certain points of the story, the film would stop and the actors would take over on a makeshift stage set up in front of the screen. Parts of the picture were set in a cinema, being attacked by creatures from another planet. Sometimes the hapless audience would find themselves attacked by the very things they were seeing on the screen, often being sprayed with fake blood and being tied up by the monsters.

The film was eventually banned because once during the infamous 'Chainsaw' sequence, twelve members of the audience were killed by a space alien who had been in the bar instead of concentrating on the action.

FINE YOUNG CANNIBAL GOES TOO FAR

When eighteen-year-old student Navin Akash, from the University of India, was on a geography course at Jaipur, he was bitten by the Krite, a deadly snake.

He had been digging through some undergrowth with his hands to try and find a particular plant when the reptile struck, biting deep into his left hand. 'I had no knife with which to cut the wound and suck the poison out,' he said later. 'And I had very little time before the poison began to take effect. There was only one thing I could do.'

Using just his teeth, he managed to bite off his entire hand at the wrist, thus preventing the venom getting into his bloodstream.

Akash then had the problem of getting back to his basecamp, twenty miles away. So to build up his strength, he ate the thumb off his right hand.

Since that adventure, Akash has also eaten his earlobes and most of his toes. 'I can't help it,' he says, 'I guess I must have just got the taste for it.'

OK, GUNTO . . . POW FROM THE LAND OF THE RISING SUN . . .

Japanese heavy metal band, Oki Gunto, who had a big hit two years ago with the song 'My Heavy Lover', decided to have a new high-tech light show for when they played live.

Last year the five-piece band made the decision to invest in a new lighting rig which, amongst all the other effects, would have six lasers to create impressive futuristic patterns.

Unfortunately for Oki Gunto, to save money, they bought lasers from a company specialising in second hand and slightly soiled equipment.

The first concert on their tour was at the Takayama stadium. In rehearsals, the lighting performed spectacularly, particularly during the opening song when lead vocalist Shirone One directed the main laser at the sky.

But when the actual performance began, it all went horribly wrong. For when Shirone stood behind the laser and turned it on, the slightly soiled machinery didn't quite work as intended. Instead of projecting a beam forwards, there was a massive blowback which instantly vaporised Shirone's head.

NOSE PICKING MADE EASY

There will soon be a cheap and easy alternative to the 'nose job', which is the most popular type of cosmetic surgery in the world.

Nias cosmetics in America have invented a device called the 'Nose Shaper' which works on the principle of the domestic steam iron.

Like an iron smoothing out creases, the 'Nose Shaper' can, using extreme heat, smooth out the shape of the nose almost as if it were putty.

'It simply pushes the excess skin to other areas,' says Duncan Passage, the chairman of the corporation. 'So if you have a particularly big nose, our device, if used cleverly, can iron away the size.'

There is only one snag. The skin that has been smoothed out doesn't just disappear – it has to go somewhere.

'So your collar size goes up five or six inches,' says Passage, 'What do you want from us – miracles?'

The company are also working on a 'fat iron' which would push unsightly bulges in the stomach down to the ankles where it is less visible.

AN INVITATION TO CRIME

According to writer Robert Webb, in Canada's *Sun* newspaper, an invitation to watch a movie for free sounds like a great deal – until the film fans return from the outing to find their homes empty. Apparently a burglar is going to the expense of buying film tickets and sending them to homes he wants to rob with a letter supposedly from the cinema announcing the give-away to promote business. While the recipients are watching the movie, their houses are stripped of furniture, television sets, videos, stereo equipment and jewellery.

BLIND WOMAN
UNMASKS RAPIST

A blind woman's ability to read braille helped police nab a rapist. Instead of feeling raised dots, the victim read her attacker's face. By keeping a cool head during her horrible ordeal, the woman cleverly felt for identifying marks on the attacker while she was being savagely raped. The manoeuvre paid off and she discreetly brushed her fingers across a distinct scar on the man's face under his eye. She later identified the man when he was held by police for questioning.

MEN PERSPIRE, WOMEN STINK!

The magazine *Weekly World News* carried out a bizarre experiment and found that women have stinkier armpits than men. Their experts say men perspire most heavily on the upper chest from eccrine glands that secrete only salts and water. Women perspire most heavily under the arms from apocrin glands that secrete salts, water and fatty substances. Bacteria digest these fats and their byproducts make sweat smelly. The result . . . women's armpits stink more than men's.

PYTHON SWALLOWS BABY GIRL

This story, by reporter Christopher Luke, first appeared in various American publications:

'A frantic father turned a horror story into a fairy tale with a happy ending when he hacked into pieces the giant thirteen-foot python that swallowed his baby daughter whole and rescued the screaming infant from the huge serpent's belly. Miraculously, the child escaped from her hellish ordeal without serious injury.'

A MIND-BLOWING EXPERIENCE

According to Irwin Fisher, police in seven countries are hunting a psychic killer – a man who, believe it or not, murders with his mind.

Twenty-seven people have died and more will follow if this man is not apprehended immediately, reported *Weekly World News* in the autumn of 1988.

According to Police Captain Serge Nevin of Marseilles, France, 'Unfortunately we have very little to go on. The murderer goes by many names, he carries no weapons and has no motive. He destroys innocent people with psychic energy – energy that literally blows their minds.'

Police first began to think they were dealing with an extraordinary killer after the mysterious deaths of a banker and his wife in Dusseldorf, West Germany. Experts found that the couple perished simultaneously when their brains exploded from within. Another pair of businessmen died in the same fashion in Australia a week later. Investigators then learned that as many as twenty-three other men, women and children had met similar fates in Greece, Italy, France, Yugoslavia and Bulgaria over the past fourteen months.

Eyewitnesses have claimed that a weird man stalks the victims two weeks before. Now police realise they are looking for the same man.

PILLAGE PARKS

According to a report in a Snowdonia newspaper, killer plants have been attacking national parks.

Deceiving because of its beautiful appearance, a poisonous plant turns into a rampaging killer. The horrifying rhododendrons are eradicating other plant life with poison as they take over. They drive out multitudes of animals that feed on the victims' plants and predators that stalk the plant-eating animals.

The pillaging plant is wiping out some of our national parks. In fact, Dr Rod Gritton – an ecologist at Snowdonia – says 'The plant has run riot. A vast area of Snowdonia has been devastated'. And officials at Exmoor National Park have declared war on the plant.

Killer plants stalking Britain's national parks is a True Story.

BACK TO THE FUTURE

Time will stop its forward march and start running backwards in late 1989, causing history to repeat itself – in reverse. That's the mind-twisting claim of Dutch physicist, Jan Colson, who says the universe will stop expanding and actually begin to recede.

GIRLS ON TOP GET DIRTY

Command of the dirty word – bucketmouthing, cussing or whatever you want to call it – may be as important as a good command of the English language for women who want to advance their careers.

According to a story in the Benton Management Resource File in Colorado, USA, profanity or swearing is a mark of success and fosters bonding with the boys in the office for the women who do it. But cuss experts point out novices must know how and when to use it in the workplace.

And ladies, never use it in front of someone you don't know, especially a superior – let him or her take the first step. Don't fill your vocabulary with it. Profanity should only be used as an expression of disappointment or humour to break the monotony.

PIG IN A POKE ON THE RUN

Convict Pierre 'The Porker' Pillet lopped nine stones off his blubbery body so he could squeeze through a tiny window and escape from prison.

'We thought he was ashamed of his weight and was getting into shape,' said astounded warden, Jacques Menard.

As it turned out, he was getting into shape . . . but getting ready to escape.

Podgy Pierre hatched his ingenious escape scheme shortly after being sent to prison for killing a friend in a bistro near Marseilles in France. 'He body-slammed his friend to the floor,' said Warden Menard, 'and sat on the poor guy until he stopped breathing.'

When he got into jail, he was obsessed with losing weight. Then he realised he could use it as an escape ploy. The former fat man removed some bars and glass from a two-foot square window, lowered his new, thin, lithe frame over the wall and made his escape with a rope made from bed linen.

He hasn't been seen since.

MAN BITES DOG

According to the News Extra Journal, *car mechanic Warren Curtiss is in trouble with the law for biting off a dog's ear. The Hingham, Massachusetts man is charged with maiming an animal and cruelty to an animal after he allegedly chomped a chunk off the ear of Fritz – an alsatian belonging to his boss, John Thomas.*

According to witness Steven Ricketts, Thomas offered Curtiss $100 to bite off the dog's ear, but the man was just kidding. 'Curtiss took him seriously,' Ricketts said.

Now Fritz, who is missing a one inch chunk of his ear, is being treated with antibiotics to prevent infection. And, of course, he doesn't hang out with the other rough alsatians . . . to avoid embarrassment.

THE BOY WHO
NEVER GREW OLD

A story by Micky McGuire in *Weekly World News*:

The perfectly preserved corpse of a World War II pilot was found still strapped in the cockpit of his fighter plane on the lake bottom where it crashed on July 4th, 1940. The long-dead French pilot, identified by his dog tags as André Mercier, was found in the water-tight cockpit of his plane. He looked, believe it or not, exactly as he did when he died at the age of twenty-three, forty-eight years before. Something in the water had preserved his body and kept the plane intact.

'It's an eerie story,' says Paul Angelot, boss of the dredging team that uncovered the plane on the muddy bottom of the lake in Northern Italy . . . but it's a True Story.

NEWS YOU CAN RELY ON

One of our favourite sources of True Stories on 'Steve Wright in the Afternoon' is the famous American newspaper, Weekly World News. *Here are just four incredible headlines from said publication, one of which has since been made famous by the British publication,* Sunday Sport:

World War II bomber found on moon; Adam and Eve found in Asia – and she was a space alien, say shocked scientists; Alien mummy found dead – he looks like an 'ET' who never made it home; *and my personal favourite,* 'Space Aliens stole my Baby', says Detroit woman.

From the wonderful pages of Weekly World News.

SCORPION ATTACKS ARAB – AND LIVES!

Here's a story by American reporter, Joe Burger:

Anguished salesman, Saleh Al-Makhlafi, had an awful earache that he couldn't figure out, until doctors took a look and found a deadly scorpion hiding in his ear. Then, to make matters worse, doctors made the terrifying creature angry so that it stung Saleh in the ear canal and the father of four had to be shot full of antitoxin to save his life.

'What a nightmare that was,' says the shaken machinery salesman in Riyadh, Saudi Arabia. 'Nothing had ever hurt me that bad or scared me that much.'

Doctors eventually removed a four-inch, killer scorpion from his ear.

AH, POOR RENALDO, SHE KNEW HE'D SWELL

In one of the more grisly, bizarre and gut-wrenching murder cases in recent memory, a cruel and conniving woman fed her cheating husband a bowl of blood-sucking leeches disguised as snails, then stood there laughing as she watched the slimy parasites drain the life from the tortured man's body.

Homicidal wife, Clarita Gomez (40), has been sentenced to life imprisonment after confessing to the murder of her thirty-eight-year-old husband, Renaldo, using a dozen leeches as her weapons.

'He was thrilled when I told him I was serving escargots as an appetiser,' Clarita explains. 'He had never had them before.'

Little did he realise he'd gobbled down these hideous, wormy leeches. He collapsed on the floor as they ate him from the inside.

PATIENT LIVES – DOCTOR DIES

A doctor dropped dead while performing a hysterectomy and a surgeon had to be flown in from forty miles away to complete the operation.

When Dr Robert Williams (54) suffered a fatal heart attack, two poverty-stricken rural Alabama counties were left without an obstetric gynaecologist. Williams delivered about seventy babies a month in Bullock and Maken counties. So when he dropped dead while performing a hysterectomy, a surgeon had to be flown in to complete the operation.

" TODAY WE LOOK AT THE FEMALE BODY!!!"

TEACHERS STRIP IN SEX LESSON

Two shapely young teachers were fired because they went overboard during a sex education class and stripped in front of a roomful of first-year students.

'I couldn't believe it,' said Anna Diaz, a teacher who was monitoring the class. 'Thank God they didn't go all the way.'

Testimony at an enquiry in Osorio, Brazil, revealed that the teachers, Maria Calbressi and Maria Vincenti, stripped to the waist in front of the wide-eyed kids and revealed their breasts and belly buttons to the children.

Mrs Diaz said she jumped to her feet and ordered the teachers to put their clothes back on, despite cries of 'Get 'em off' from the male members of the class.

SEX CAN MAKE YOU SNEEZE

People who sneeze after sex aren't necessarily allergic to it, says a new study in the journal of the American Medical Association.

'The sneezing is probably due to vasomotor rhinitis – a fairly common syndrome in which the nasal passages are chronically inflamed,' said Dr Jeffrey A. Wald.

'The condition is characterised by hyper-active or im-balanced control of certain nervous system responses. Vascular tissue in the nose is similar to that found in the male sex organ,' said Dr Wald. 'Sexual arousal may cause swelling of the mucus membrane inside the nose and an increase in nasal secretions.'

So that's why you sneeze after you've bonked.

SCIENTISTS SOLVE A WEE PROBLEM

This story is from the Singapore Gazette:

Singapore scientists have developed a method of catching thugs who urinate in lifts. They've fixed up their lifts with a chemical sensor which reacts to the scent of urine. The censor then activates a video camera and stops the elevator between floors, setting off an alarm.

'HE'S BACK – AND THIS TIME IT'S PERSONAL'

Scientists have found a way to produce super-strong bullet-proof vests out of spiders' webs.

British researchers at a company called PA Technology discovered that the extremely strong silk spun by spiders is excellent for absorbing the impact of fast-moving bullets. They first noticed the material's amazing usefulness when they observed flies hitting webs at high speeds. Now they've devised a way to produce the web silk through genetic engineering and include it in their famous bullet-proof vests.

DOG DISAPPEARS – OWNER DISTRAUGHT

This True Story has been donated by BBC TV personality, Phillip Schofield. He tells me of a true story he heard about a woman who took her lovely fluffy white dog down to a West Country headland, only to misplace the animal and discover a yapping head bobbing up and down in the choppy sea below. Utterly distraught, the woman called her dog's name again and again, becoming even more upset as it looked as if the head was disappearing underwater. Suddenly she heard barking from behind her, even as the white figure in the sea yapped louder and louder. The dog didn't jump – the figure in the sea was a seal puppy.

ET LETS ONE GO

Author, Rupert Matthews, tells an unusual UFO story. In his recent book, *UFOs and Aliens*, he explains that unidentified flying objects do not often give off an odour. When they do, it is almost always unpleasant. The strange craft seen at Blenheim, New Zealand, is typical of the UFOs which do smell.

On the morning of July 13th, 1959, a woman was milking her cows when she noticed a green glow all around her. She looked up and saw a huge, circular object coming nearer. The woman ran to hide behind a tree.

As she watched, the UFO came down to within a few metres of the ground. Through the clear dome on top of the craft, the woman could see two figures dressed in silver suits. They seemed to be examining the controls on their craft. Then, without warning, the craft suddenly shot straight up into the sky. It left behind the stench of burning pepper! It was hours before the smell eventually disappeared.

NOT A LOT OF
PEOPLE KNOW THIS

Michael Caine, the film actor, always a man for a True Story, reminds us of a scene featuring an obvious mistake in the classic, The Sound of Music, *in which Julie Andrews and her charges are in a market. Visible under a stall is a crate containing Jaffa oranges, on which is written 'Produce of Israel'. 'Pretty damned good,' says Michael, 'considering the film is set in the 1930s during Hitler's rise to power and the state of Israel was not founded until after the war.'*

SEEDS PLANTED IN TUBS – AND THEY ALL LOSE WEIGHT

America's *National Examiner* reports this wacky tale:

There is a new diet fad in Thailand where hundreds of fatties swear they're losing weight by sticking seeds in their ears. The bizarre treatment is used at Bangkok's Yan Hee Polyclinic, where diet guru, Dr Supote Samritvanitcha, tells his patients to attach lettuce seeds to a bandage and press them against an acupressure point in their ears ten times before each meal. His patients swear it has helped them lose weight, but experts warn it's actually dangerous and that the real reason patients are losing weight is because of the appetite suppressants the doctor slips in their drinks.

MACHO MEN LOSE OUT

Women become lesbians because men aren't tender enough, said the United Nations last year. A UN sponsored report implied that if men treated women with tender loving care, fewer would turn lesbian.

It said the assertion of supposed male supremacy has had a deeply disturbing effect on many women, and that there would be fewer lesbians if men were able to be more affectionate, more attentive and more tactful.

COPPER SNAPS ALIEN, FOUR FEET TALL AND GREEN

An ex-policeman claims to have taken a photograph of a frightened space creature, says a top British UFO researcher. The creature was four and a half feet tall with two long arms dragging on the ground, according to ufologist, Steve Ballen. Ballen told the *Yorkshire Post* that the ex-policeman showed him the photograph and that the alien had big ears, huge staring eyes, no nose, smooth bright green skin and no visible private parts.

GAY DOC IN SEX SWOP OP

This story is from Richard Dominick – a respected American journalist:

  A gay doctor, who loved his wife but couldn't stand living with a woman, performed a home-made sex-change operation on his sleeping mate. 'She was shocked, dismayed and screamed like a Banshee at first,' reports Richard. Dr Julio Lopez, the gay doctor in question, claims his wife calmed down when he told her how much he loved her. Now the doctor's wife, Maria, is apparently a fantastic man named Garcia – good looking, with black whiskers and a moustache – thanks to the home surgery.

REDS UNDER THE BOG SCARE

This story is from reporter Ragan Dunn:

Soviet scientists claim to have found the mummified remains of no less than six hundred space aliens in a peat bog in Northern Siberia. 'This is the scientific discovery of the decade, if not the century,' Dr Gennardy Charlamov told reporters in Moscow.

'The proximity of the remains to those of sabre-tooth tigers and woolly mammoths suggests that the aliens arrived on earth at least thirty thousand years ago. We have yet to find evidence of a space vehicle, but that merely indicates that the ETs were teleported to earth.'

The experts' theories have played to mixed reviews among Western scientists, some of whom think Dr Charlamov is raving mad.

IT'S A 'MIRACLE' – GIRL SURVIVES DEATH

An eleven-year-old girl was dead for twenty hours and miraculously came back to life seconds before astounded surgeons were to remove her vital organs for transplant. 'The life support machines had been turned off,' said Dr Filipe Akuete. The girl, Shireen Locken, of East London, South Africa, had been declared dead. Doctors kept her hooked to a life support system for twenty hours so that organs due for transplant WOULD NOT be damaged. Then a nurse noticed three fingers on her right hand move. The nurse ran through the hospital shouting, 'She's alive, she's alive – a miracle.' Together the surgeons, nurse and patient got down on their knees and praised the Lord.

LOVE TRAP COUPLE PREMATURELY EJECTED

A young couple went to see the movie *Blow Out* starring John Travolta and were so bored they decided to make love in the back row. Unfortunately, the young woman's internal muscles contracted just a little too much, jamming the couple together. Luckily, help was at hand. The cinema manager was able to prize them apart with a large crow-bar before giving them the biggest ticking off of their lives. You can understand why we've left out the names and places on this particular one.

WARNING SHOT IN THE HEAD

Believe it or not, just eighteen months ago the intense heat of California drove otherwise sane people to shoot other drivers. For a month during 1987, LA highways were plagued by freeway shootings. If, for example, a lorry driver overtook at high speed and cut in front of another car, he would be shot in the head. This happened at least five times in what became known as 'drive-by-shootings'. Experts blamed the intense heat and humidity in LA that year.

NO MERCY FOR
DIRTY DOZEN

A Mr K. W. of Cleveland, Ohio, wrote to the 'Sound Off'
column of America's *Weekly World News*:

Dear Sirs, I read the story about the slasher who had
sneaked into cinemas and killed twelve people while
they were watching gory horror movies on the screen. I
say, go get 'em, man. Anybody who would pay their
hard-earned money to watch people get chopped to
pieces in a movie has to be sick in the first place, so I don't
feel sorry for them getting their throats slashed. Whatever happened to good, clean entertainment like those
old Doris Day movies? If people were watching those
kind of films, they wouldn't get their throats slashed.

LAST-MINUTE SAVE AT LIVERPOOL

A sixty-one-year-old woman underwent emergency surgery after a dried apricot snack swelled up like a balloon in her stomach. Doctors said that the dried fruit concoction absorbed certain stomach juices when swallowed and the apricots reverted to their original size within a day. In fact, her stomach grew to the size of a football, and doctors at Walton Hospital in Liverpool were lucky to save her.

BUTCHER GETS THE CHOP

A butcher screamed in agony when he sliced off all five of his fingers on his left hand with a butcher's chopper. And, believe it or not, he collected his severed fingers, put them in a bag, went to his local hospital in Detroit, Michigan, where, during eighteen hours of painful surgery, doctors successfully reattached them.

BABY GROWS IN A BOTTLE

Restricted space and a fine on families that have more than one child in China meant that new-born Fok MaJing was hidden in a large earthenware bottle from birth. As he grew, he began to take on the shape of his container. Now aged twenty-three, he is two feet tall and has an eight-inch-tall neck.

'I don't hate my parents for doing this to me,' he said recently, 'at least I stand out in a crowd.'

THE NOSE ALWAYS KNOWS

Incredibly, the fairy tale of Pinocchio seems to have an element of truth for forty-four-year-old Ian Simpson of Britain.

Whenever Mr Simpson lies, his nose grows longer, and if he tells several lies simultaneously, it can grow up to three inches in size.

'It's a real pain,' he said recently in a local paper. 'I can't even tell a little white lie, like telling my wife I've only had a couple of pints at the pub. She only has to look at my nose and it tells her otherwise!'

Doctors investigating this strange phenomenon believe that the increase in size is a result of nervous tension causing blood vessels to expand. Simpson's nose contains a unique type of cartilage, which is more flexible than an average person's.

'I don't care what the reason is!' he fumed. 'How would you like it? It's not even as if all the exposure I've been getting due to it has earned me much money!'

Mr Simpson's nose increased in size at that point.

DRIVER GETS AN EVEN BREAK

You wouldn't have thought that a broken ankle could be in any way beneficial, but it saved a man's life.

The man, who does not wish to be named, was driving past a building site when a car shot out at high speed from his right. Mr X slammed on the brakes – and got a different sort of break!

'I felt my ankle break,' says Mr X, 'and I knew that I couldn't put the car's brake on. Luckily, despite the pain, I managed to steer clear of the other vehicle and use my other foot to stop several yards down the road.'

But the drama wasn't over. For at that point, a cable snapped on a crane lifting some heavy blocks of concrete and they plunged down onto the road at exactly the spot where Mr X's car would have stopped, if not for his ankle.

'I couldn't believe it!' he says. 'But I'd rather have a broken ankle than no ankle at all!'

ASHES TO ASHES . . .

While spraying his armpits with deodorant, Terry Marks of Seattle accidentally dropped his cigarette into the spray, igniting it and incinerating himself within seconds.

At least he doesn't smell any more.

LOYAL IN LIFE – AND DEATH

Many people are aware of the loyalty of pets, and cases are well-documented of animals staying by their master's side when they are ill or in danger. But one of the most extraordinary cases was that of seventy-two-year-old Katherine Bell of Michigan. Mrs Bell owned twenty-four cats and eleven dogs, to keep her company since the death of her husband some eleven years before.

When her mail began to pile up and she didn't answer her front door, neighbours called the police, who sadly found her dead. Incredibly, though, pathologists also discovered that every single one of her pets had died at exactly the same time as Mrs Bell. Animal telepathy of the highest order? We'll never know, but it's probably the ultimate act of loyalty, and another True Story.

STAR OF THE SILVER SHEEN

Dennis Harding, a Texan on holiday in Mexico, found himself tortured by toothache and unable to find a local dentist. So, to ease the pain, he constantly drank ice-cold water which deadened the nerves.

However, the pains got worse, and one morning Harding was astounded to find that his teeth had turned silver overnight.

When he eventually reached a dentist, he was told that the high concentration of zinc in the local water had built up on his teeth, creating a silver sheen – but the dentist was unable to remove it.

So now, Harding has a new job. He advertises toothpaste, as his teeth really do sparkle.

HUMAN CANDLE SNUFFED OUT AT LAST

Jimmy Braithwaite's party trick was to eat six wax candles while doing handstands. When he died and they cremated him, it took twenty minutes for his ashes to burn out.

EGG-CLUSIVE! BOY HATCHES OUT

Recently, the chief of an African tribe claimed that one of the pregnant women under his care had given birth not to a child, but to an egg.

Although doctors say this is impossible, the woman has undergone strict lie-detector tests, none of which give any indication that the claim is untrue. The woman says that the egg was about forty inches in diameter, and when it finally hatched, a normal healthy boy emerged.

The child, who has not been named for privacy's sake, is now three years old and appears to have feathers instead of hair. Doctors are keeping a close eye on his development.

POSITIVELY
LEGLESS

Losing both legs in a strange cooking accident seemed like the end of the world for keen sportsman, thirty-year-old Terry Exley of Canada.

But what seemed like a handicap at first has proved to be beneficial in a quite extraordinary way. Exley himself takes up the story in the magazine, Canada Now: *'I was depressed at first, obviously, but then I thought – why let this get the better of me? Life has got to go on, hasn't it? So I invested several thousand dollars in some very special artificial legs.'*

Exley now has a collection of eight pairs of custom-built false legs, all specially designed for different sports, including legs with built-in water skis; legs with built-in flippers; a pair with ice skates attached; and one pair that form part of a racing bike.

'These legs are, in many ways, better than normal ones. I mean, I don't have to do up complicated boots or anything and I never get blisters,' he says.

THE PASSAGE OF TIME

After Tibetan monk Dai Cho Lama fell over while playing a nose flute, the instrument became lodged in one of his nostrils. Doctors are unable to remove it without causing worse damage, so now the man talks only with musical notes.

THE GREAT
BANANA SKIN
SLIP-UP

A Brazilian footwear company has shocking news for all makers of comedy films, for the soles of its new line of shoes are based exactly on the structure of – wait for it – banana skins!

Their tests, they claim, have proved that the skins do not have a slippery effect at all, but in fact grip better than rubber.

The shoes are not yet available in the UK, but when they are we'll be 'falling over ourselves' to buy a pair!

A WELL-GROOMED MAIDEN

We all know that men can play terrible tricks on the prospective groom at his stag party, but none have been quite as bad as the jape played on Brian Cohne two years ago.

Unknown to Cohne, the fifty friends he had invited to the party had all put $100 each into a special fund, and when the party began, they set about plying poor Brian with as much alcohol as possible.

When the twenty-six-year-old finally passed out, he was immediately taken to a very special kind of hospital . . . and the money was handed over.

The following morning, Brian woke up with more than a hangover – for he was no longer Brian . . . but BRENDA!

His jolly mates had arranged for the poor lad to have a complete sex change, and of course, the wedding had to be called off.

Two years on, Brenda remains philosophical: 'The lads were always larking about, so I should have realised something fishy would happen. You've got to see the funny side, haven't you?'

Brenda is now happily married to the best man at her original wedding.

TREE SIGNS

On the coast of Venezuela there is a tree that screams. The tree, dubbed the 'Ugly Screamer' or 'El Janis Joplin' by the local populace, is full of naturally formed tubes and diaphragms. When the coastal winds blow at night, air is forced into a large knothole at the top of the tree and pushed through the tubes, to emerge at the base of the tree through a mouth-shaped orifice as a long, low scream.

MISSION
IMPLAUSIBLE

Daring Japanese improvisation comedian Spikes Harvey Yamamoto died in a shining example of improv comedy. He would ask his audience to suggest a stunt for him to perform on stage. 'Nothing is impossible,' he would say. One night, someone told him to ski through a revolving door. The stunt was a success, allowing for the fact that Yamamoto emerged from the door in six slices.

100% SPOOF?

Scientists in Las Vegas, USA, have developed an intelligent drink that talks. Local members of Alcoholics Anonymous are given bottles of the liquor, called 'Old Strangeways', as a form of aversion therapy. When poured, voice circuits in the bottle attempt to convince the alcoholic not to drink. If this fails, the bottle will scream horribly, as if in abject agony, when drunk. Jeremy Gittenburg, who has now kicked the habit, said, 'It works great. How can you drink anything without remembering the death rattle of Old Strangeways?'

ICE-CREAM KID LICKS TOWN

Experts investigating this next true story tell us that they believe it to be 'a bit dodgy'.

The small South American country of Almenica is currently under siege due to a brilliant scientist and his seven-year-old son. The scientist, according to rumour, had invented a machine that could, quite literally, create anything the operator could picture in his mind.

He found his young son looking sad and offered him the first go. The lad, who had just been refused an ice-cream by his mother, created a regiment of indestructible robot soldiers that vaporised his parents, took over the country and constructed a huge pipe to supply the lad with ice cream.

Yes, we agree, it is 'a bit dodgy'.

THE STUN NEWSPAPER

Australian heavy metal singer, Jonna Hangerou, died in very strange circumstances indeed. His mother had died the day before, and Jonna had not yet been informed as he had no telephone in his house. But he was found dead, slumped over a newspaper that carried an account of her death. Some thought that the shock had killed him – but Jonna was blind.

THE HUMAN JEWEL CASE

The mystery behind one of the great jewel thefts of history was recently solved. In 1931, Sinead Causeway stole the priceless Knight's rock. Pursued by police, the mentally unbalanced woman went to the home of her mentor in crime, Edward Bargeld, and stabbed him almost to death. The police arrived and doctors saved Bargeld's life. Causeway was executed, but the jewel remained hidden until 1980 when Bargeld finally died, and a post-mortem was performed. Causeway had shoved the gem into one of Bargeld's wounds, and the Knight's rock had lain behind his collar bone for fifty years.

DOG BEATS RAPE RAP

Los Angeles police raced to the home of elderly heiress Mrs Gloria Vanderbilt when she said her little girl was being assaulted on the lawn outside her home. They had a shock when they discovered that the 'little girl' turned out to be a poodle.

'That horrible man next door,' said Mrs Vanderbilt, 'put his horrible fat mongrel on my lawn, and it . . . it had its way with Fifi (the poodle).' Mrs Vanderbilt attempted to file a lawsuit against the offending canine, but police thought it would be 'a bad idea'.

KENTUCKY FRIED BRAIN

Professor Jake Keraki, of Kentucky University, believes that aliens have invaded in the form of briefcases. Keraki, currently 'under observation' in the Kentucky home for the sadly confused, says, 'I saw them at the airport, on the wheels, following each other like ducklings. And I saw them asleep on conveyor belts. They obviously have an agreement with airport authorities. We must make contact with them.'

The principal of Kentucky University declined to comment.

MEN WILL FLY
BEFORE PIGS

In ten years you may well believe a man could fly. Pioneering surgeon, Dr Jameson Slodeth, claims that in the next decade he will have the technology to perform the impossible, by splicing together the genes of humans and eagles to produce flying men. 'I will be able to build angels,' says Dr Slodeth. 'But on the other hand I may just produce people with big noses and lousy haircuts.'

MATCHING EYES

In the eighteenth century, scientists believed that eating matches would help you see in the dark. They thought that the phosphorous in the matches would get into the bloodstream and increase the amount of light in the eye. Sadly to say, advocates of this theory died horribly of poisoning.

SECRET LET OUT OF THE SANDBAG

A seventy-two-year-old Frenchman, Pierre Callin, has studied for over half his life under an ancient Chinese master in order to achieve excellence in the hitherto secret art of underwater sand juggling. Little is known about this difficult and obscure discipline, except that one is required to hold one's breath for up to six hours at a time. Callin has acquired, according to reports, the 'Black Coral' – the highest level.

Seems to us a bit of a waste of time.

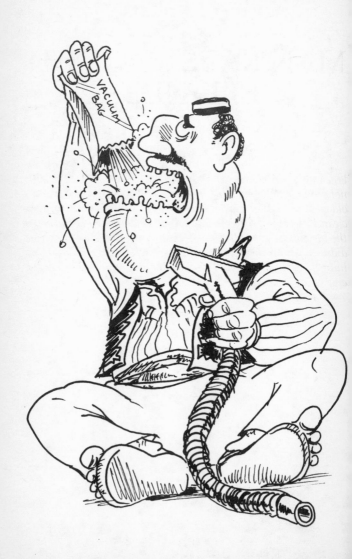

MAN EATS VACUUM CLEANER

Unemployed Albanian, Khriss Brett, was utterly destitute with not a rouble to his name. All he had was a room, a bed, and an old vacuum cleaner. So to ward off starvation he ate his vacuum cleaner. Doctors, who are at a loss to explain how he survived the metal meal, say, 'He must have a cast-iron stomach. If he didn't, then I'd lay odds he has now.' Khriss shrugs it off: 'I was hungry, that's all. I would've eaten the bed, but I couldn't fit the end in my mouth.'

BAD LUCK OL' SON

The musical fad of 'Acid House' is bad for your health, as proved by Acid House fan, Justin Opper, from New York. He tied his bandana very tightly before he visited the club, then he drank and danced a lot and the heat expanded his head. He refused to take the bandana off, and just after midnight, his head exploded. The body was not removed for two days because the DJ felt it 'added to the decor'.

GETTING OFF ON
THE RIGHT FOOT

Adele Gordon was given a novelty soap on a rope by her boyfriend, in the shape of a foot. She took a wash with it, and found her bath full of white paint . . . and a real foot on a rope. She went to visit her boyfriend to ask him to explain the sick joke – and found him walking with a stick. As a token of his undying love, he'd cut off his right foot and given it to her.

FROG FINED

French university student, Jean-Marc Jammer, loved causing trouble. One day he found a copy of the university charter dating back to the sixteenth century. In it, he found that according to a 300-year-old university law, he should be served a glass of port in lessons, so he gleefully demanded his right. The principal acceded, and went to read the charter himself. Jammer left the lesson, cheerfully replete, and was fined one hundred francs for walking across the quadrangle without carrying his sword.

SHOULD WE TELL
EDWINA?

Carpets are bad for you. Expert A. E. Vanne says that all carpets contain the chemical Selkiephrine 102, and if you walk barefoot across the same piece of carpet twenty-four hours a day for 192 years, you will die of carpet poisoning.

DIY PROJECT GOES HORRIBLY WRONG

American Poul Herberts was the unluckiest man in the world.

He was building a partition wall in his kitchen when he heard a shout from outside. He turned round, brick in hand, and put his weight on his right foot, which was merely a stump after an accident two months before. He fell over, his head landing in the microwave oven; the brick hit the side of the oven, dislodging a safety circuit; his other hand hit the 'on' button, and his head was vaporised.

OLD BLUBBER FACE BOWS OUT

Impressionist Jimmy McFingus performed his last act in 1981. He impersonated a whale while performing at a Japanese Seamen's Convention . . . and his impression was so realistic he was set upon and slaughtered by the harpoon-bearing audience.

ANOTHER FISHY TALE

All dolphins are alcoholics. Dolphinologist Jennifer Nikohol states that oxygen has the same effect on dolphins as alcohol has on humans. This, according to Nikohol, is why dolphins make 'those silly burbling noises'.

Nikohol was recently admitted to hospital suffering from 'exhaustion'.

THE INVISIBLE MEN

A little-known fact about World War II is that the American naval research department discovered invisibility. In 1943 they rendered an aircraft carrier, the Abigail Cable, *utterly invisible off the coast of Philadelphia. An unexpected side-effect of the invisibility, however, is that it caused the entire crew to go blind. Radar couldn't pinpoint their location, and the* Abigail Cable *was never found. Somewhere on the high seas an invisible aircraft carrier may still be drifting.*

LOOK VIDAL'S AT IT AGAIN!
HE'S MISUSING THE TARGETS!

A SHARP PRACTICE

Did you know that scissors were thought to have been invented by an ancient French tribe? But not for cutting!

The blades were forced into the ground and the two circular handles were used for target practice, the idea being to get the arrow to pass through the 'eyes'.

It was only much later that some 'sharp'-witted genius realised their cutting potential.

BOGEY MAN
BUMPED OFF

*Picking your nose is a horrible habit, and Jeremy Port of South
Africa picked his from a very early age.*

*However, both he and his family thought it would stop when
the twenty-four-year-old lost his hand in an accident at work
and had it replaced with a hook.*

*But as soon as he came out of hospital, he attempted to have a
go in the ambulance on the way home. The vehicle hit a large
bump, and the hook went straight up into Jeremy's brain, killing
him instantly.*

"THE END IS NIGH!!!"
OR IS IT?

BONKING BAN ON BLOND BOMBSHELL

Here's a true myth from Sweden!

According to legend, in Sweden lives the ugliest man in the world. The tale says that if he should ever lose his virginity, the whole planet will explode. So ladies, if you're ever approached by an incredibly ugly man with blond hair . . .

THE LAST SUPPER – LEFTOVERS FOUND

Dr Peter Broom, an American archaeologist, claims to have found the remains of the 'last supper' of Christ. Broom claims to have found the remains of a house nearly fifteen feet underground in an area where the biblical event was supposed to have taken place.

As a result of intensive research and tentative theorising, Broom has ascertained that the leftovers weren't bread and wine at all, but a primitive version of lager and the Doner Kebab!

Other archaeologists are not impressed. Four years ago Broom claimed to have discovered the core of the actual apple that fell on Newton's head, leading to the theory of gravity.